Take Your Hand Out of My Pocket, Shiva

Take Your Hand Out of My Pocket, Shiva

Leonard Gontarek

Hanging Loose Press
Brooklyn, New York

Published by Hanging Loose Press, 231 Wyckoff Street, Brooklyn, NY 11217-2208. All rights reserved. No part of this book may be reproduced without the publisher's written permission, except for brief quotations in reviews.

www.hangingloosepress.com

Printed in the United States of America
10 9 8 7 6 5 4 3 2 1

Hanging Loose Press thanks the Literature of the New York State Council on the Arts for a grant in support of the publication of this book.

Cover art by Catherine Gontarek

Cover design by Marie Carter

ISBN: 978-1-934909-89-8

Library of Congress cataloging-in-publication available on request.

Acknowledgments

Barnwood: "Philadelphia (Caveat)," "Zen"
Blood Orange Review: "Study / Pond," "Study / Early Summer"
Coal Hill Review: "Love Poem," "Homage," "Toward Fire"
Fogged Clarity: "Ways Of Mourning"
Handsome: "Nighthawks," "Edward Hopper," "Evening Snow"
Hanging Loose: "Grace," "Crow, Scarecrow," "I Know," "Pretty Rain,," "Innocence"
New Purlieu Review: "Black Lines"
Press 1: "Tabloid Story" "Interior Place," "Late December Light," "Untitled VI,"
        "In Winter," "Early Summer," "Sasha Grey," "Park," "November, Early"
Scythe: "Mid-June Lament"
Skidrow Penthouse: "The Past," "On Love 2"
The Straddler: "Middle Of October IV," "Night," "Spring V," "Landscape & Car"
Verse: "From Grace"
The first line of "Calico" was lifted from Philip Schultz.

CONTENTS

Grace	9
Philadelphia	10
March	11
Crow, Scarecrow	12
8 AM	13
I Know	14
Pretty Rain	15
Love Poem	16
Homage	17
The Park	18
American Landscape	19
Zen	20
Tabloid Story	21
Estate	22
Toward Fire	23
From Grace	24
Interior Place	25
Escalate Peace	26
Evening Landscape	27
Calico	28
Woodsmoke	29
Self-Portrait with Door	30
2009	31
Locust Trees	32
Late December Light	33
Untitled VI	34
In Winter	35
Evening	36
Hotel Insomnia	37
Innocence	38
Fall	39
Ways of Mourning	40
Nighthawks, Edward Hopper	41
On Love 2	42

The Past   43

Evening Snow   44

Study / Early Summer   45

Study / Pond   46

Mid-June, Lament   47

Middle of October IV   48

Night, Spring V   49

Landscape & Car   50

Madeleine   51

Sasha Grey   52

Goddamn Kings   53

Philadelphia (Caveat)   54

Park   55

Morning Snow   56

December Snowfall   57

Early Summer   58

Warm Night   59

Of Silence   60

The Stars   61

Broad & Locust   62

The World Goes Down to No.10 Pond   63

The Change   64

Black Lines   65

Nights in April   66

Religiously   67

Philadelphia Is on Fire   68

November, Early   69

Torn Light   70

Party   71

Prayer   72

For Muriel Rukeyser and Mark Strand, in memory

"Take your hand out of my pocket, I ain't got nothin' belong to you"
—Sonny Boy Williamson II

GRACE

A restaurant afire.

Right? Windows rattle. Meat cooks.

Fine rain falling. I stand outside it.

A cat chases fragment of dark in darkness.

Think *you* can break my heart?

PHILADELPHIA

Night coming down,

the way a waitress calls you *Hon*.

MARCH

My garden is green.

My neighbor's has bloomed

small yellow crocus

in a cluster. *Punks.*

CROW, SCARECROW

A crow sits on the head

of a scarecrow. I see myself in that.

Which part of *fuck off* don't I understand.

8 AM

The soul smokes in secret.

The soul hates his enemies

and those he loves.

I Know

I know it will be winter soon,

the dark blooms

in glazed landscape and zero weather.

But it is summer,

you spread your legs

and my glasses steam.

Pretty Rain

The pretty Asian woman stands

on her tiptoes to fix

her take-out coffee.

And it is raining.

How long are

haiku supposed to be again?

Love Poem

I erase the penciled name on the front page

of the book.

I can still see the ghost image of the letters,

can trace the shape pressed into the paper.

Tell me again why you left me.

Homage

The last time I read this poem

publicly, I was drunk,

standing on a table,

and I went home

with the prettiest woman at the party.

The Park

Those young men in the park, in camouflage clothes—

what is it they want to disappear into?

AMERICAN LANDSCAPE

A car pulls up in front of a bakery.

Two women get out, brush each other's hair,

and go in.

ZEN

I wanted to be purified.

I called up Gisele.

We took the car to be washed

and stayed in the car and screwed

under the large, sudsing brushes

and hot, pulsing jets.

Don't you think

that was an excellent solution, Master?

Tabloid Story

I started to laugh, so people would think

I was crazy and they knew

the reason for my craziness.

There was no other explanation.

I named myself after the baby

and swallowed a packet of begonia

and zinnia seeds. America can be dark

and its soil warm, holding flakes of mica, rust, and

that damn dusk that won't go down.

ESTATE

Faraway. The tools in the workshop in the adjoining yard

of childhood: here mysteries are created and mended.

This yard, this lovely yard, with fish heads for fertilizer.

The pets are buried. It's close to autumn.

Toward Fire

Could it have been twenty years ago the hearse

drove by filled with oranges?

Wind in trees as though they were catching fire.

Give me, you said, *tonight, another night.*

I gave you ice water. Rather, the ice from the water.

FROM GRACE

I may force the soul into nakedness.

I may lead the soul around on a leash.

I may dress the soul in women's underwear.

Which part don't you understand?

I did not win the Hemingway look-alike contest again this year.

I could pass for the Polish President & Prime Minister, I think.

I've painted myself into a corner here, away from the cobalt galaxies.

For another, I've cut a door in the wrong wall to get away.

Interior Place

Pray, on your knees (where else?), for rain & a big bag of food from,

say, the Fifteenth Century. Under the fuchsia, where you are getting crappy light

in the garden. Kick in the ass. Put on your witch's hat & start already.

Trees, you must leave the house by dawn, or we will trail you like ghosts.

And you don't want that.

ESCALATE PEACE

They flake & disintegrate, those tiny black seeds in the flower.

Terrible thought. Could die without her.

The only path to the Divine he knew

that was not mined with fools, wolves & party firecrackers.

The sea: *Hear it cursing in oblivious black.*

Flashes of nightbirds or crazy moonlight, alone.

Evening Landscape

There is something scary about the children's games.

The neon hopscotch at dusk. The way

everything rhymes, or seems to.

Is this about you? It is about tenderness.

So, yes, perhaps.

CALICO

I dicker with God.

He takes me at my word.

The calico's head is cocked

to the right, listening to Puccini.

Sleet. Only silverware going

through the spray of the washer.

WOODSMOKE

Woodsmoke, today, filled me

with such longing.

Spread your legs

like Jesus' message, for me.

Self-Portrait With Door

I entered it, many times.

The light and door flaked away

like brittle pages of an old book.

The field was always on the other side,

a fairground before the sun rose.

The crows were the only ones happy there.

And, sometimes, without make-up, the clowns.

2009

The young want to see constellations.

They see an even green and orange sky past midnight.

They couldn't be sadder if their poets

were unable to write in symbolism.

Locust Trees

In my poor country, we poured sugar

on everything to not notice our hunger.

In spring, the shining coats of blackbirds

were turned gold by sunlight.

The locust trees were thick with petals,

but many had fallen to the ground.

Our neighbors lay scattered on battlefields,

some literally rose into heaven.

LATE DECEMBER LIGHT

Someone has stolen the baby Jesus.

I wish I were home.

In the mess of connections of trees,

I wish I were home.

A tiny lake of summer light.

Unfolding cloud.

Flowers come,

from the tintinnabulation of the ground,

they come.

Untitled VI

Tulips & snowfall of dogwoods in the cemetery.

So it is.

I spike the lemonade with whiskey & mescaline.

Gulp it down, drink my face from the river.

I ain't gonna sit in no backseat of spring like some bitch, Lord!

In Winter

An odd light, it is.

They kiss long in the driveway of a church.

They taste like lifesavers to each other.

EVENING

You open the doorway into dissolving leaf-light

and I go with you, amen.

There is a woman and a man reading

and eating in the sepia window.

Flickering silver, one hand passes through water

to another.

HOTEL INSOMNIA

The music carries muffled into the trees.

The heart's a mouser, let's not kid ourselves.

INNOCENCE

The ice cream truck jingle drives my sister crazy.

I wonder if they have vanilla.

FALL

He was the class clown.

His uncle died.

He came back serious,

as though Death had scared off

a circus act of mice from his kitchen with a broom.

WAYS OF MOURNING

My father takes me out of school early.

I'm 9. Mother is dead.

He lets me drive.

NIGHTHAWKS, EDWARD HOPPER

I would go home with you,

but you are going to be famous,

and anyone knows

loving a famous woman

is like the flake of bird heart

ants swarm over.

On Love 2

The woman was talking about how she had maybe

three cigarettes a week now, cut down from twenty

on a good day, while the barista ground into earth

my French roast. She wasn't with me, she was with

the other guy in line. Yet I was lost in

the death sentence of the down-to-her-ass fairytale hair.

Just as I was surprised by autumn moments before,

though it had been autumn for days.

THE PAST

I used to frequent seedy movie theaters.

I don't remember the names of the films,

they probably had sex in them.

I don't remember what the movies were about.

I remember something of what I felt

and who I was.

I loved this young man.

I want to smooth his collar with my hand,

easy to do, since sometimes they left the lights on.

EVENING SNOW

The snow is old. My neighbors

put old furniture in it

with a broken drawer. Warped records.

This way and that way in the drift.

Soup comes from the house.

Soup comes from the house like pink twilight.

Cats and students are drawn to it.

As you wish, seek God.

Study / Early Summer

All day, long dark cars have pulled up in front of the house.

Weeping women have been led out & in.

The elders fan themselves with pamphlets,

sneak whiskey into their lemonades.

Study / Pond

Blacktop shines.

Mystery is overrated.

I fuse to what I see, Lord.

Fear eats a plain doughnut.

The field shorts out, Lord.

The undersides of leaves are lit & wet.

Meditation is given over to ants & myth.

We swam & screwed & swam

& smelled like water, afterward, Lord.

Mid-June, Lament

We want Hell. And why not, it's summer.

The wind rustles the beaded curtain of the sycamore.

There's a graduation party suave with Christmas lights

and an electric keyboardist rushing through the Barry Manilow songbook.

The extremists want Limbo.

God is tied up like a babysitter.

Middle Of October IV

I am the only one in the outdoor café.

The leaves rush across the stones like birds.

It is cold here where I am in shadow,

warm in the corner where light drapes the tables.

God, there is always one waiter, one more thing to do.

Night, Spring V

I want to talk to you, directly.

Who knows what to say?

My face floats like a mask

on the creek that courses under the houses.

The roaches are big as dogs, almost, and hiss.

LANDSCAPE & CAR

A contract between light and the junked orange cars.

The earliest, tv moon past dusk, my dear.

A covenant between first sex and dark love afterward.

Dew oils the woods. We gulp each other.

Unfortunately, it may be always like this.

I am sorry, it is possible. No one knows who owns this place.

Creatures come and go, freely. The roof riddled with stars and bullets.

Madeleine

If you don't love me,

the terrorists win.

SASHA GREY

Be the porchlight to my mosquitoes.

Goddamn Kings

We can walk around the garden

like goddamn kings, but neither the word nor the objects do we own,

if we own anything,

The drizzling light & beast on a leash,

invisible, mythical,

eats from our hand.

Philadelphia (Caveat)

Prayer is dark coffee, little milk, lots of sugar.

It occurs only at evening, which is now.

Park

Okay, we get the idea,

pigeons love breadcrumbs.

Morning Snow

Winter has drifted in and around the abandoned church.

Remember the smokers gathered outside on the sidewalk?

Wonder what they talked about.

December Snowfall

The reader is asked

kindly to correct in the text

all references

to the colour plates according

to the List of Illustrations.

EARLY SUMMER

It rained in the country,

splashed on the letter.

Originally, night-ink,

the precision handwriting

turned hydrangea-colored.

But what is the garden,

but a dream after all.

And, the insects, ghosts, if they exist at all.

Warm Night

The houses land in streetlight.

The garden becomes full of flowers

and the hose drips.

Before dinner is over,

spring is going to have to tell us

who the blonde whore is she was kissing.

OF SILENCE

The moon slides behind a cloud, darkens the edges.

My neighbors like to talk outdoors.

The lawn chairs creak.

They lift the King of Beers from a chest of diamonds.

Insects and tree frogs own the night world.

In impaired, incandescent language, they argue the point.

THE STARS

Lord, I did not shoot Bristol Palin

dancing with the stars on television,

my living room reflected in the glass

rattling like pie tins and sheriff badges.

It is about time. Indian Summer

negotiates the tequila aisle

of the liquor store, slightly drunk

with a shopping cart, Lord!

BROAD & LOCUST

The dead step to the back of the subway & down you go.

Heck if it isn't a demon whispering in your heart.

Apostrophe of blood at corner of its mouth.

Snow & fire sliding from leaves of the night trees.

THE WORLD GOES DOWN TO NO.10 POND

By which I mean, the light.

The world is a hundred years old.

The photograph, level with the world.

The world is sepia, drenched in dark.

Silver flakes from the oaks.

The heart is a black phone in the attic.

Dog running around for no reason.

Before you know it, panes of light fallen in the grass.

The Change

The surface of America is set afire.

I'm talking about the sea of wheat.

By midnight, the stars are

green and blue, metallic.

I shake when I hear *The Pledge*.

My shoes are restless in the sawdust.

Death and blood and lies of omission

are a perfume, inexpensive, an intoxicant, I tell you.

Black Lines

The site is slanted, black lines of rain, in the garden, as you see it.

The site is growling trees, near power line.

The site is black river, stars, junk, red sofa.

The site is afraid of getting close, like any good site.

Let's revisit: Target is curdled cream, tea, Spanish for petal.

Search: The target is a boy, explosive terribly made, around his pet's neck.

The site is drenched in spring. Who would name a cologne Undertaker? The president.

The End is all white, ripped-up pipes, smoke, snow, an arrow of shadow loose.

So, it is April, evening. This is what a broken heart looks like.

Nights in April

Black cat eating

softly in darkness.

Two young women smoking clove cigarettes

on a porch.

Sorrow, we will not become you tonight.

Religiously

In the morning, when

the clouds are pouring down,

I'm pixilated,

hungover from X-Files, E.M. Cioran, Asian porn.

I bow to the earth

to gather a fistful of electricity from my cat.

Philadelphia Is on Fire

And we've just finished making love.

Our bodies soaked.

The engine siren dies down.

Another one starts up in the distance.

From the curtain, look, august autumn trees.

November, Early

In Buddhist terms, low self-esteem is an illusion,

but the accompanying sadness and ache

is pretty real. I think this early dark throws us out of whack too.

I'm sorry, probably the only remedy,

and it's temporary, is to rest your head on someone's chest in a cemetery.

Light favors the gray area.

TORN LIGHT

If the world smells like rain in the morning

and it does not rain.

Nothing latches on to almost everything.

In the morning, the birds settle like soft taps

of erasers on blackboards.

The chalk breaks and skreaks.

PARTY

There was the custom of placing

all the guests' coats

on a bed. I went home,

tipsy, with a kitten in my pocket.

This New Year's Eve

I buzz-cut a hip heart on my cat's side

and I got a tattoo, a large anchor

on my back. I vow never to drink darkness

again, I know, a promise impossible to keep.

Prayer

Slate gray clouds gather to

the gold pond in morning.

Shall I pray for spring,

rooster heads of flowers

pecking their way above ground?

You are number 5 in the queue.